*DISORDERLY MAGIC
AND OTHER DISTURBANCES*

Richard Cabut

www.farwestpress.com

First Edition

ISBN 979-8-9858067-5-5

Printed in the United States of America

Photo Credits:
Cover and back cover – Richard Cabut archive. © Richard
Cabut.
Page 12 – By and © Gregory Hesse. Triptych arrangement by
Richard Cabut.
Page 25 – Richard Cabut archive. © Richard Cabut.
Page 26– Richard Cabut archive. © Richard Cabut.
Page 34 – Richard Cabut archive. © Richard Cabut.
Page 62 – Richard Cabut archive. © Richard Cabut.
Page 64 – By and © Gregory Hesse.
Page 70 – Richard Cabut archive. © Richard Cabut.
Page 72 – By and © Richard Cabut.
Page 90 – Richard Cabut archive. © Richard Cabut.
Page 91 – Richard Cabut archive. © Richard Cabut.
Page 105 – Richard Cabut archive. © Richard Cabut.
Page 106 – Richard Cabut archive. © Richard Cabut.

CONTENTS

FOREWORD

By Sylvie Selig, artist, Lyon Biennale 2022, visitor at Warhol's Factory.

I want to live inside these poems.

INTRODUCTION

By Richard Cabut, author.

Disorderly Magic and Other Disturbances is a pop meditation on a number of themes: speed, delirium and distance, disillusion, urbanity, various manifestations of the idea of the wilderness and the wasteland, madness, dissolution, memory, mourning, forgetting, hauntology, hauntings, rapid transits, the non-existent, and conjuring the future.

It is dark jazz, post-punk, post-pop verse. Essential beat-up/down, free-fall, free-for-all poetry for people who perhaps don't particularly like or think about poetry (and for those who do, of course).

The work mixes magic, culture, mystery, memoir, history, melodrama – it is an invocation, an evocation, with dreamlike freedom of movement between past and present, from personal to universal.

This underpins explorations of fate, bewitchment, nostalgia, loss and home – culminating eventually in my own intensely personal interaction with a past, the essence of which remains elusive. Worlds and words that are desperately fragile – mapping the loneliness and expression of private sorrows (on the edge of being pinned down by our own ghosts).

The work amplifies explorations of: emptiness, aimlessness (artistic and otherwise), different manifestations of the experience of alienation and isolation, capturing the importance of historical context.

Cultural touchstones which and who bear witness, include pop art (blankness), Rimbaud, punk rock, post punk, Patti Smith, Ballard, Witkiewicz, Beckett, Witold Gombrowicz, Polish and European cinema, (the philosophy of) pessimism, and grief – 'We must really believe in the ruins (of our memories)'.

There are also clear cultural references throughout the work – from the Velvet Underground to French film.

The aim is to transform/reconstruct the sense of the world as the unfolding connections between people, events and places remake its pattern.

For

Danuta Cabut (1951-1973)
Ludomir Cabut (1925-2005)
Czesława Cabut (1930-2020)

We are enveloped and steeped as though in an atmosphere of the marvellous; but we do not notice it.
– Charles Baudelaire, *Salon de 1846*

Now is the time of departure. The last streamer that ties us to what is known parts. We drift into a sea of storms.
– Ariel, *Jubilee* (1978), Derek Jarman

Who wants to be an angel?
– Ingrid Superstar, *Chelsea Girls* (1966), Andy Warhol

The magical night is not close to dissipating.
– Benjamin Péret

Deep looks good on me.
– *Will & Grace*

PREFACE/BIBLIOMANCY

When I was younger –
one of Marek Hłasko's
'beautiful twentysomethings'
– perhaps/perhaps not –
I would invariably,
before starting to write
a review,
a poem,
a story
or a song,
pull out a book
from the shelf
at random.
Open it arbitrarily.
And place my finger on the page with
eyes closed.
To find a word
as signifier
and *mojo*.
A form of bibliomancy.

Now, once more, for *Disorderly Magic...*,
the book I have randomly selected is
Man Bites Man
by George Ives,
the word I have excavated:
Justice.

Just is.

Asymmetrical balance.

As it should be.

Atmosphere – how to get back to zero

DISORDERLY MAGIC

There's a Negative Girl
down the tubes.
She leans on the wall
that someone has just spat on,
green w/luminous yellow flecks.
Colour of her aura.

The girl looks like she's died
but doesn't know what to do next.
An apparition.
She's listening to music.
Shit music;
it doesn't matter.
Green gob on her clothes;
it doesn't matter.

In the café,
a guy big ears
looks at
a guy big mouth.
Agog, believes he'll
say bouquets
of words.

Oh, guy big mouth talks ...
destroyed by madness...
... boredom and bad luck.
Stripped raw,
craving, neurotic.
Ugh.
I feel sick listening to this.
My body is falling apart
in slow motion
but accelerating all the time.

The streets stink.
The door of my house is
cracked.
So is the street.
The world is made of odour,
trauma and
wise cracks.

Wise wounds, too.
Life as anxiety dream.
Scrambled with a tall-tale joke.
No kidding.

A can left on the wall
that someone has slashed in
for the winos to drink –
and then spit out, splutter...
and laugh, resigned.
It's canned laughter.

It's a cosmic joke.
Sour pissed-on dreams.
On the never never.
On the never ever.

In N London, angel-headed poet
is sectioned.
He has finally achieved madness;
*The only performance that makes it
all the way.*
Am I right? Eh?

Once upon a time in Soho,
amongst the everyday overnighters,
broke 'n' starving angel head was given
money for sustenance
by artist F Bacon *none other.*

The first time Bacon saved someone's bacon.
Maybe/maybe not.

Now angel poet takes ECT in the wards,
and Dharma Jack, the bum, says:
the first sip is joy
the fourth is madness,
 the fifth is...
... ecstasy.
Am I right? Eh?

ECT angel poet says to electric musician
who visits him:
You are not here
because I killed you.
I will kill you again.

In mad dreams death is just an aside.
Part of the rhythm
if not the rhyme.
Angel poet does
not speak again.

Ex-toothless writer, up West Way, is on his Nth
nervous breakdown.
Though he tried he just can't hide his eyes edged with
tears.
But at least, he thinks, nervously,
I am better off than her:
what a state.
Not solid: fluid.
Floating.

She dreams, in her cups,
of a bathtub as big
as a swimming pool
to get pissed in.

To piss in.
To piss off.

The painter, lying on the floor, says,
I just feel so fucking horrible,
haven't felt this bad for twenty three years.
I got up today with such fierce horror on me. Ah.
Fierce horror.

The careless carer, also West,
Takes doctor's pills for bitterness and regret,
Lives on Facebook, self pity
and green and yellow spit.
Singing sad Country and Western.
Yee ha.

In strange flat,
the photographer is picked up
and thrown
against the wall black and blue
by grinding lover's
drug dealer.
Should I leave? He asks himself.
Only of my senses, he decides.
Crumbling empire of the senseless.

Same photographer has a particular mania.
He can't walk over bridges
for fear of the fall.
He says, *yes, well, but we'll cross that bridge*
when we come to it.

I don't know but I've been told,
those who aren't certifiable now
are on the waiting list.
It's ready to swallow us all.

Publisher by the sea
mentions casually, the rot, urbanity and debris.
Unflinching, so real it leaves you feeling
and tasting the filth,
the uncouthness of it all.
Oh, the *uncouthness.*

Man, he continues apace,
I've seen this, witnessed it, been chained to it.
Lived it. Fathomed it. *I am, oh God, still living it
and surrounded by it,* this life...
... *the circumstances.*

Vile, yet alluring, wearisome,
comprehensive in the imaginable certainty
of this or that kind of lifestyle and...
... *oh no... yes... really?*
... reality.

In south London sauna, another cuckoo
already flown over the nest.
Psycho-ceramic, cracked pot.
No need for a Rorschach test,
this guy,
just some super glue.

Smiling, fit to melt, rising heat,
dreadlocks hanging, swaying.
He says, I drank three
Wray and Nephew a day.

I couldn't get what I want.
Desire.
Desire is the devil
– beat Buddha style.

I used to see thing, he says.

Delusion illusion monsters
speaking in fiery tongues.
My friend filmed me,
posted it on social media
for laughless laughs.
Delusion illusion monster.

Every night, a horror cinema
plays in my head, he continues apace,
slasher shit,
running on the beach,
footprints sinking underneath the foam
like stars blowing up.
Escape blurs into something else
– there is no obvious pursuer.
There is no one
there.

The other photographer can't escape
the chaos and wonders:
but what if all the symbols and numbers
in people's lives –
as though they are all just characters in a poem –
this poem maybe –
all add up to empty fiction?
No feeling, no meaning.

But pure poetics
is meaning,
the transcendent mainline
to the soul.
I'm searching for my mainline
I couldn't hit it sideways.

And people's lives,
meaningless to some,
especially to themselves,

are pure poetry, too.
Boundless in and out of their depth.

dimwits and dum dum boys,
street prophets, aesthetes,
type writer throwers, charlatans,
wanderers, situationists,
phonies, sophisticates,
crooks, imposters,
tricksters, sign writers,
alchemists, stumblebums,
born losers, flaneurs,
dopes, no hopes.

And just like author Janet Frame,
I am not really a writer:
I am just someone who is haunted,
and I will write the hauntings down.
I will write them
all down
and out.

I am just someone who, like everyone, is
looking for some magic.
Dirty magic.
Disorderly magic.

And this poem is a spell.
A drive in.
A dive in.
An evocation,
an invocation,
a charm,
a bewitchment,
and a way of conjuring the future.
A way of conjuring the future.

I'm looking for the invisible.
Unalloyed feeling
and heavy hymns,
strange energy from the streets.

In the fold of the city
I bump into
F Bacon's mate,
the Devil – just like Bulgakov never happened.
He is human after all
– a devil one moment and an angel the next.

He says:-
Have some marrow in your lost bones,
bleached in the winter sun.
Strung white around your neck,
swinging while you walk,
still when you talk.
Write it on the walls of your heart
while waiting for the lights to change.

But I am in a hurry.
I am looking for a kiss.
Looking for a snake
wrapped around my wrist.
Looking for a story
that doesn't end in disaster or doom,
or that fizzles out, like most,
in deathly gloom.

So
it feels exactly like rebellion, just having
mad sex on a broken bed, shattering it –
break it up
break it up
break it up
– breaking its thin-sprung stained mattress.

And after, just throw it out on the street.
The streets are made of
fucked on fucked up fly-tipped mattresses forever.
Fucked on fucked up fly-tipped mattresses forever.

In the diamond frost and eventide
the sky lowers itself down on to the streets.
After lifting her skirts, the sky penetrates the streets
– the streets cry out – ah –
and the sky covers her completely. Almost gently.
When the sky comes, it is from the depths
– from all the way back – from
a different, previous, time.

The streets never sleep, but still dream.
The streets dream
and so do I.
A dream is always a dream within a dream.
Oh yeah?

At night everything changes.
The moon is made of tears and
the sun is made of stars,
in orbit while we
throw shapes and shades.
Shapeshifters and shoplifters.

Cursed bedsit, cigarette burned floor,
shit marked bog, lighting tubes flickering,
last gasp,
greasy cooked chicken,
ancient cock and cunt magazines piled high,
lager foam crumpled cans,
multiple locks on dirty door, menstrual smell.

In the fog.
London,

St Leonards,
Warsaw.
Grey street,
afternoon growing colder,
dusk silver white.

The writer lights a candle
in small shrine
to Beckett in
his bedroom.
And burns the whole house down.
It is worth it, he thinks;
the sublime.

The collar of his jacket turned
up against the wind.
Freeze frame.
French New Wave.

But life isn't a movie.
It's a selection of blurred, half remembered
Polaroids –
self pic amateur porn, dead people, blank mis-shots –
scattered on cigarette burned floor.
Existence as *Kodak crack up.*

Poet, but not angel-headed, sits at typewriter
Clack clack clack.
Eternally, rips out, screws up
words and flings them on floor –
a magical mountain of crushed paper dreams.
A poetry of the failure
to write poetry.

A writer can rewrite his life.
A poet can re-rhyme her verse.
And beautiful dreamers can

reimagine their desires.
Vagrant visions –
here for a flickering second, a minute,
a second minute, and then gone for good –
there is no such thing as lost time
and stolen time is sweet theft.

Piss drenched potholed bombsite
dossers walk barefoot in rubble
like actors on Shakespearean stage
seeking authentic connection with the
boards they tread,
walking on slivers of broken bottles
As if on tightropes.

But the power of the performance,
the only one that really makes it,
is rooted and booted
in that which is not an act, or pose.
A kind of moment that
baked its shadow into the walls
and only now the sound is fading, if ever.
Am I right? Eh?

On the wasteland someone on knees gives
blowjob to someone,
head bobbing.
Onlooker is transported
to uncoiled extended time.
The future is felt in the throat like a gasp.
Sperm in radiant arc.

Unkempt magic and stolen kisses
For nobody, or nothing,
Not even the rain...
I love the temporary.
I know all about life.

I know that everyone betrays everyone.
But you and I.
You and I will be different.
We will always find each other.

We will
Always
Find each
Other.

Set in full moonlight, before the Flood

Passage of a signal, dilation of the pupil

DREAMING'S ENGLAND

There is more than one England.

One is made of motorways, inner-city car parks,
out-of-town malls, mobile phone masts and
hyper speed.
Everything, even ir/reality, commodified,
and transactional.
A vast cold space.

The other England is
buried,
hidden,
naked,
crouching somewhere deep beneath.
This England is made of
desire,
magic,
jouissance
– the chance
of happiness beyond
fucking shopping.

We love art that uncovers
the seething spiritual world
underneath the temporal one –
we are all excavators or palaeontologists.

Insouciant visionaries following
mad logic.
not just mind blowing, but delineating
– epiphanic beauty.

A complex tale.
For what is a community
without the stories

we tell ourselves about us?

Not all is rosy in this
psychic landscape
– it's not, and never was, Eden.
Myth can also harm if it's used only to fortify
against the truths of a situation.
But, this deep, wild England also contains
the euphoria of possibility
which mingles with our dreams.

IN THE CITIES

Anomalous shops,
flats above,
graffiti-ed and lurching towards and away
from one another,
as though frozen
in the act of collapse
– like blackened teeth in a mouth
repeatedly punched.

Carnal nature of brutalist council estate
articulating concrete.
With energy of fucking,
repetition and invisibility.
Solid magic algebra.
In which all answers
are known but unremembered.

All made in the night.
Identified in dark.
Unrecognised and abandoned in the day.
The night helps to heal the daytime trauma
with garbled myth and experience
like an abstract ambient music –
sound system mix.
In day there's only sunlight to play with.
Everything wound tight.
Up tight.
The days don't end
fast enough.
The sun can be wished
right out of the sky.

Slow transits
fast distance.
Angels brushing commuters'

eyelids with their wings.

Station to Playstation.
Haunted zone cheap film noir.
Smeared moon bent chimneys.
Plotting in alleys.

Passers'-by halos
seen only on CCTV.
Heliocentric art,
Kirlian photography,
society stripped down
naked,
raw electrical discharge.

Everyone waiting
in hush of dim buildings
for...
the blow, or just blow,
or to be blown
and, blown away –
frivolous profundities,
bringing us closer to
our hushed-up, eternal selves.

Waiting for
something that
forever happens somewhere else
to someone else.
Cities are where people learn
to dwell apart from their desires.
In city centre,
carved blocks
and solid statues
with unflinching
24/7 stony gaze at
street life

overwhelmed by images.
Cities always tell stories of ourselves.
Underexposed expositions
of exits as existence.

Screech of tyres
and metal.
All civilisation
is in
driving seat.
Automatic transmission.
Smooth.
Red zone – max revs.

Distant energy
but always
close up.
Up close
inverted fear.

Smears of neon
flickering bodies
angled bedsheets
heavy sweat.

People living in cities to
be
alone,
avoiding themselves,
especially their own shadows.

Living in
join-the-dots
abstract.
Pre-packaged
impotence
– TV snacks while

the adverts are on.
The adverts are *always* on.

Somewhere the internet stops working.
Somewhere it is raining.
Somewhere blood appears on sheets.

Resting in the
fabric and weave of the commonplace.
Outside, a trashed old couch,
springs uncoiling,
nestles in the corner of
waste ground.
Small black cat slinks
through stinking evening.

Fractured dialogues,
fragmented discourse.
Concentric rings of entry level anguish.
Random anger that
affixes itself to a sense of tiredness
and default sickness.

Delicate malice – cold yet involved.
Soullessness as service industry.
And every instant in history,
at this or that ongoing moment,
is a flash of unequalled
desolation or
unparalleled joy.

Motionless, dehydrated,
glowing – toxic hallucination – always beneath
the surface.
A bad energy envelops everything.
And people wear masks forever.

And streets are crowded
with ghosts of gods and goddesses
who cut off their own heads.

And a small figure squashed
by that *infamous* scale of towers,
highlighting the idea of
great perspectives
and towering frontages –
sparkling promises which can
never be realised.

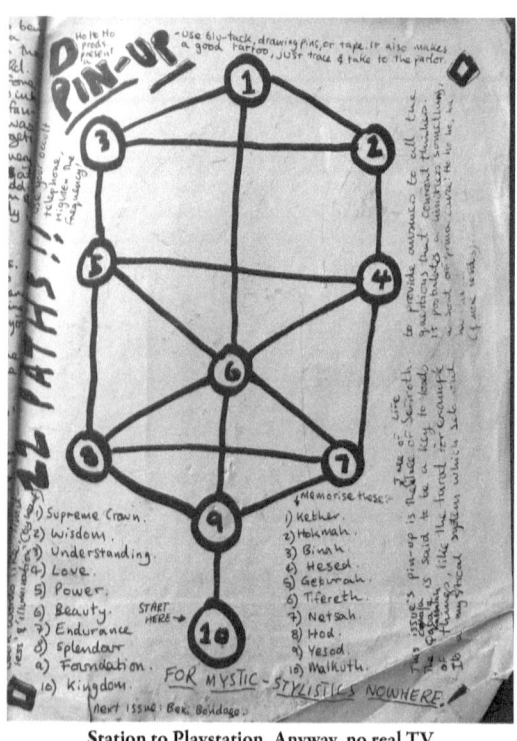

He Ho Ho predix present in the...

PIN-UP

- Use blu-tack, drawing pins, or tape. It also makes a good tattoo. Just trace & take to the parlour.

22 PATHS!!

telephone, might be handy

to provide animals to call the questions that connect thinking. If it prohibits "memories something like a bird or green cord. He he he he he.
(if you wish)

Memorise these:
1) Kether.
2) Hokmah.
3) Binah.
4) Hesed.
5) Geburah.
6) Tifereth.
7) Netsah.
8) Hod.
9) Yesod.
10) Malkuth.

1) Supreme Crown.
2) Wisdom.
3) Understanding.
4) Love.
5) Power.
6) Beauty.
7) Endurance.
8) Splendour
9) Foundation
10) Kingdom.

START HERE →

This issue's pin-up is the Tree of Life composed of Sephiroth. It is said to be a key to load things, like the hand, for example. Anyway, like the hand, for example, magickal system which is set out...

FOR MYSTIC - STYLISTICS NOWHERE!

Next issue: Bex. Bondage.

Station to Playstation. Anyway, no real TV

TENTH FLOOR

Conversation – compressed
and fragmented.

Tube. Elephant & Castle – White City.
Artificial light.

(Talking wicked about: technology and heart/
Fiction romance has happened,
is happening,
will happen/
night, and travelling through/
sometimes there's nothing else
– 'Yeah, we got it all covered.'
/Langston Hughes' *Freedom's Plough* – Hold On,
just hold on...
/Paranoia/
Mishima – Acts of Worship and other forms of glam
negativity/
Tai Chi and actually manifesting the energy which
remains as a glow/Boston, Mass. – a life of TV
basketball, rock music and weekends in NY/hatred
of nostalgia.)

Silence. Walk. White City Station
to nearby flat.
Red moon.
Wet footsteps, cries in the night,
whistles and a high flat geography.

Song. Taxi.
White City to Aylesbury Estate.
Headlights. Words are falling.
Can you see the rain... ?

Dream. Aylesbury Estate, south east London.

Flash light.

Airtight, airless, self-sealed,
dedicated to producing a new nervous system,
dreaming the dream of the Holy Barbarian:
of how youth culture is good
but the idea of survival is better;
an immediacy which
hits every day.
From 13 to 30
along 22 paths and beyond.
Beta-punk.

The place I am speaking about
is damned up for good with the
crosswire barriers that
burn and hum.
Tenth floor and it really is
a neon wilderness up there.
Supra-beatnik dreams.
Talking about Neal Cassady's abandoned wife
and lost love that screams silently
like a supersonic whistle.
But it's better than jerking at the flailing of useless
limbs
as the disempowered drop sheer down into the void.
Expressions not even set with terror
and violent shock.

Neon?
Akin to the '60s chrome; all Sputnik red
and spunking up the night sky
with voluptuous bearings.
A dim star in isolation with
nerve endings feedback black:
evocation with the end of evostikschtick,
gluing and pounding together

all the crazy parts that add up to the whole.
Where live all the dogs, agog (and vice versa).
Where the world's forgotten boy
can twirl around his head a luminous bar of light
and hit shadows reflected in no other's face.
Like a star?

No, not at all.
From A to B.
But fast,
so that the edges are sharper;
the type of charisma that only sustains
itself at fifteen hundred miles
an hour, or so.
And home is really some bar full of stevedores,
merchant seamen,
prostitutes.
A flow of verse comes via
a drunken dandy who is ready
with tongue and fists,
like some crazed Rimbaud.
When poetry and atmosphere merge,
the excitement is almost equal to
that of a dazzling crime.

(I'd rather steal antiques than work in an office
or wherever/
speaking easy to the friends uptown/
dropping into the underground /
dropping up – block out the blockdown/
here's to the friends of the underground/
and the friends of the friends of the underground.)

Which goes in the vein like a dose of alchemy;
golden, a real vision.
Into space – the space and pattern between words
and

music where there are only pretty
funny shapes stretching out.
Flailing the wires for extra frenzy.
Gold, except that this serpent shines without
glittering
– the eye of a tuneless moon,
climbing the chimney stacks along the 22 paths
that lead to right here and now.
Where the world's forgotten boy can twirl around
his head the luminous bar of light
and hit shadows reflected in no other's face.

THOUGHTS WHILE WATCHING *CHELSEA GIRLS* AT THE SCALA CINEMA, LONDON, ON SATURDAY 10TH SEPTEMBER, 1983

I know the Chelsea Girls.
They are everywhere
in my life.
In my wife.
They're climbing out of the silver screen
and over the Scala seats
into the filthy Kings Cross streets.

Others climb into the dirty screen
to take their place.
Split screen psychosis.
Coiled circuitous energy –
we are all wrapped up in foil.
It really is *enough to make you sick*.

The Chelsea Girls are in my
spiky blue black hair.
They are in my flat.
In my pants,
my imagination,
my dreams.
In my kitchen, drinking my instant,
no milk, ta.
Stealing my cigarettes
and speed.

Chelsea Girls are in love
with the narcissism
of youth.
They'll *be your mirror*.
J'adore the beautiful silver fast forward
and divine boredom.
Beatific beat up ennui.

They say: 'Everything.
Every colour is electric.'

Chelsea Girls are in the Wag Club,
spilling my drink, relaxing
into the deterioration,
with a little desperation.

Unheroic missed chances,
emanating unflinching insincerity.
They smell of the isolating sense of sadness
and queasy premonition.
Runny blue black mascara,
grey wash on cheeks.

They laugh at the thought.
Mirth that filters
through cigarette smoke
– St Moritz or French,
mon cher.

Chelsea Girls are cold.
Sadistic – like the randomness of... *everything*.
They disappear into the starry night
like the fine design on a fading portrait.
Get the picture?

Chelsea Girls drone nihilistically
or with an agonising shriek.
A flash of aural filigree – seamy quality,
redolent of hot tea,
greasy gin and stained carpet.

Chelsea Girls are thin, eating only thwarted love
and psychic torment,
regurgitating contempt
for everyone.

At dinner they chew on
liberated beauty.
At breakfast;
degraded claustrophobia.
Food for thoughtlessness.

They wait for something to touch them.
You've always gotta wait.
Forever falling down winding stairs in high heels.
Eyes set alight with feelings
they will never share.
Get your own.

The Chelsea Girls are fat on ill luck
and no prospects.
But they are better than *you*.
Unhappy solitary heroes
of the 20th century –
1982, 1983, 1984!

They say: 'I never knew where I came from,
could have been *a mansion or a shack up*.'

Chelsea Girls always know how you feel
– they sharpen their claws on your mood.
Their minds are jolted and honed
and rendered almost clairvoyant
by disorder.

They say: 'Oh, it was just a demonstration
of options, nothing more.'
Nothing more.

Chelsea Girls have white faces puffy with alcohol.
And spiritual decimation.
It would always be like this, they are sure
– this dull little screwed up video

of life with its never ending
abeyance of miracles.
It would simply get worse.
Pffft.

The Chelsea Girls have orgasms all the time
– their best climaxes are not defined by bliss,
but by worldly defeat and the need
to inure themselves against it.
As compensation for... imperfection.

They say: '*Oh me*!
Oh dear!
Oh my!'

Chelsea girls prefer flesh to aura.
They give and get blowjobs while chewing
gum and smoking cigs.
Full of pornographic reels,
the Chelsea Girls blow hot and cold.
They fellate consciousness
and unconsciousness – or, so they say.

They love the smashing of everything,
the wear and tear.
Kicking and screaming.
All the loneliness of the world
is in tantrums and tears.
They wear it well.

They go only to places
where ugliness
is anonymous.
Their facades
contain so many signs.

They say: 'And I can't tell good fortune

from bad
anymore.'

The Chelsea Girls hate
second hand sadness
and the sorrow
of the second hand.
And the old.

They say: 'In two years' time, baby,
I'm going to dance
out of the window
ten storeys high.'
They've been saying it
all their lives.

The Chelsea Girls are all Catholic
and think aesthetics
is the drug to a sense of damnation.
They say, while looking at their reflection:
'I am a state of grace.'
While touching themselves.

They want to touch themselves
all the time,
but not too profoundly.

The Chelsea Girls live in a warehouse,
factory or hotel,
where innocence and viciousness,
are interchangeable.

They live in the jewelled,
black underground
because underground life
can offer clues and traces
if it is occupied wholly.

Down, down.

Their leather glamour is rooted in
the meditation on flesh,
and ruinous passage of time,
the dissolving of the self,
the unworkability of everyday life.
They paint their toenails red.

They affirm: the transitory radiance of display.
Image in and out of focus.
Pout of focus.

The Chelsea Girls are a divine investigation
of the urban night.
In the daylight
they hide in the shadows,
but only their own.

Youth, narcotics, art, allure, chic.
Flattering disorientation,
self-admiring carelessness.
Viva!

Their parents own Julie's in Holland Park,
and the Portobello Hotel, too.
One day they will send the Chelsea Girls
to the States on drug cures.

Chelsea girls fuck in the toilet
of the Portobello and
jack off in any restroom.

Their sex life is a feeling between
the thighs,
like a cornered cat.

Their parents are factory workers
and industrial cleaners
who will not touch this mess.

Chelsea Girls drive
old green Morris Minors,
and snort
philosophy of art.
Sniff
psychology of beauty.

They discount the premise that
Concept
is as substantial or insubstantial as
Feeling.

They say: 'I'm just your style.'
All just words strung together,
strung out and strung up.

They transform their time
into a single *pure* instant.
They write party invitations.
Never sent, and not to you.

Chelsea Girls never think about:
teenage prostitutes, poverty,
strikes, poor education, abortions.
Well, sometimes the prostitutes.

Chelsea girls don't write
or admire books.
Only films and videos,
set in public lavatories
and nostalgic mansions.
Although they never read books,
they read something into everything.

When they make films,
the camera is as still as a corpse.
Hand held/hand job.
Jump cuts. Tracks on arms. Tracking shots.
From roof of sportscar.
Shooting movie shooting speed.
Metallic silver brilliance of arc light.
Camera settles on ineffable unreality.

Chelsea Girls are not poets of the dispossessed
but they debase themselves
in pissoirs and swimming pools
for *art*.
Films so dejected that the inferno
which inevitably ends them
comes as sweetest relief.

Probing motion and visage
within flames within frames.
Primitive alignment,
the element of the form creating other forms,
more or less airless,
intertwining out and in,
and elsewhere.

They say: 'I want to be as interesting as
the inside of an ordinary toilet bowl.'
They are driven by emotional ambition.

Soundtrack: '80s pop, Bartók
and the Rolling Stones' *Emotional Rescue*.
You will be mine,
you will be mine,
you will be mine,
all mine.

They read *Story of O* and *The Image*

out loud to other commuters
on the tube.
And they look at horrible Soho porn
on the crowded bus.

They believe in the brilliance
of their own fabulous mode of life... of existence.
The Chelsea Girls adopt a certain aloofness
when dealing in
the unfathomed zones of the spirit.

Hanging out with suicide drag queens.
Beauty, madness,
and loss creates a novel kind of appeal,
slurring the lines between dearth and art.

They say: 'Imagine a world without us!'
Imagine!

Chelsea Girls are the experimental film that
they themselves have been waiting
to participate in all their lives.
Not so much a narrative as a Spectacle –
in state of perpetual deterioration.
We're not into films.
What then? Chaos.

The Chelsea girls say they are the most
garish baubles on the charmless bracelet
of *youth*.

They throb and vibrate with holiness
and sainthood.
Silver Girls. Silver boys.
Saints of the town.
Naked blessedness.

Denizens of sanctity: chattering, prancing, fondling,
shooting up, putting on faces,
revealing nothing except the gravest of secrets,
smacking each other.
So holy that *anything is possible*,
including torpor.

Extreme self-absorption
is a miraculous purity,
they insist.

Chelsea Girls buy speed from dealers who do nothing
but press ups in their front room all day.
Chelsea Girls sell speed to pathetic
music press writers and editors.

Chelsea Girls live life as in a cult classic,
in excruciating dullness.
Yet it's not fair
to equate *that* with pointlessness, they protest.

The Chelsea Girls
comb their hair,
peering into a mirror and talking to themselves.
The nature of their conversation is unknown,
or secret.

They confess their sins.
All fake.
Lost words of the loveless
echoing in the endless night.

Chelsea Girls transform their negative
Scientology personality tests,
done on Tottenham Court Road,
into disordered artworks.

Chelsea Girls never answer
the phone to lovers,
and drive them madder.

Chelsea Girls are smoking cigarettes on a bed,
one is naked,
the other is fully clothed.
Every surface communicates.

Chelsea Girls take Df118s
and sleep for 16 hours.
It's good practice, they say.

They know magnetic personality
is only a product.
Going cheap in the supermarket,
or cut price in the corner shop the day after.

They believe strongly in an absence of symbolism
to provide fleeting junctures of freedom.
But don't call it stillness, they warn.
Stillness is movement that
halts performance and holds the image
in unfolding display.

Chelsea Girls work as cleaners in Hampstead
where their employers
love the *demimonde*.
Chelsea Girls are always sick
on the way to work.

They think thoughtlessly
of the poetic *avant garde*.
Modernist pure thought
while hoovering.
Martyrdom is a richness
afforded to the Chelsea Girls.

But not for free.

Chelsea Girls are not a commercial viability.
They are not standard alienation.
A subtle transaction.
Back and beyond of
the entitled charm of the drifter.
Glowing.

Chelsea Girls are
A) Filtered, seeping infrared like a negative.
B) Blonde.
C) A masturbatory trance.
D) A story without mythology.
E) A story with mythology.

They always lick their fingers,
squeeze their lips
and twist
their thoughts.

Chelsea Girls forever steal.
They are the most hardened criminals of Berlin,
Rome and the King's Road.
Their favourite art is plagiarism.
It's *the only way to be*.

The Chelsea Girls
crown themselves with
laurels and thorns
of their own cruel design.

Chelsea Girls steal art,
cheddar cheese,
books
and kisses.
Their kisses turn their lovers' lips blue.

Hot for crime,
a luxurious untruth.
Chelsea girls know only one thing,
that genius is
not an award
but an exit
for lost causes.
They know everything.

The Chelsea Girls are mere pleonasm.
It passes the time.
They say: 'I am in so much pain.'
But it is better than being plain.

Chelsea Girls come into filthy hankies
while thinking of their mothers
and the Other.
Here they come now, the Chelsea Girls.
Fashioning conceit into
emphatic transgression.

Chelsea Girls prostrate themselves to
and before indifference.
Vive le difference!

They gossip like everyone else dreams:
in black and white.
Muckrake while huddled in mute fury
in corner of every room.
Room split between grandiloquence and solipsism.
Dramas of disjunction.

All their friends are dead.
They grieve by wishing
all their other friends
were dead, too.

The Chelsea Girls are aware (self) that
sooner or later
every liaison,
artistic or psychic,
turns into a conspiracy.

Confidently spare
pose.
Strangely
stark scenes,
which capture our own image within them.
Images always denude.

They would like to think
that a doleful vision
and broken poetics
is enough to purify
the imagination.

Pale figure, shrouded, spectral amid ruins
routinely, humdrum conundrums.
Pointers to their own unanswerable queries.
Chelsea Girls are decaying
in the loft window's hot *white light*.

A long-exposure spiritualist visitation,
A way of hiding self from self – selfishly.
A disappearing trick.
Be very careful of the Chelsea Girls.
They aren't there.
Or here.

Brim with blackouts and soul shattering,
while keeping a distance from themselves.
Outside each other,
with little intent to recall,
or recoil.

Conversations into formality.
Rhythm less.
Nothing leads to anything else.
Conversation repeated.
No anticipated ending.

Chelsea Girls are a special little secret
that speaks of
the aggressive perfection
of a passive nonchalance.
With their cocks hanging out.

The Chelsea Girls walk home at 4am
from West Hampstead to Islington
in broken boots and bloody soles.

'The epic is so splendid, like myself,' they say.

The Chelsea Girls fight outside
Finsbury Park clubs because
they think that being vicious
is the first truth
in the tell all,
tell-tale mirror.

Chelsea Girls have the flavour of artists
in their mouths.
The taste of
self-communion
and upside down kisses.
The pretence beneath the matter.
What's the matter?

The Chelsea Girls drift,
seemingly on sentiment.
Their smiles look like sobs.
Incoordination displacing

the centre of perspective,
if not gravitas.

The Chelsea Girls piss
out of the window
into the sparkling
moonlight.

They are not 16 any more
but never recompose.
Recalibrated attraction
is a form of defeat. They feel.

Their old beauty is like stone
carved definitively –
it will crumble
into the powder
they themselves will snort.
Chelsea Girls are as beautiful as chance.
They are the beginning of the void.
A black hole to avoid.
Wired for sound.

Chelsea Girls are always vile.
They have neither realised
nor forsaken their desire –
freedom from either arrogance or acerbity.
The Chelsea Girls are an incomplete
experiment.

'I'm looking so *old*,' say the Chelsea Girls,
in order that others may deny it.
The looks on faces of others
reveal not the slightest pretence
that they think
otherwise.

The Chelsea Girls gesture:
'There is no poetry to be extracted
from my life – which is lived
with a language scrawled
indecipherably in purple ink.'
Only purple will do.

The Chelsea Girls say:
'Lately I've been imagining
other scenes of sublimity.'

Chelsea Girls know that anticipation
is meaningless
because there's nowhere left to go.
It's all played out.
It always has been.
They say.

The Chelsea Girls have just realised
that the stakes are themselves.
They apply the deadpan
pan stick of core cynicism.
They don't even
bother trying to exchange
integrity for frivolity,
or vice versa.

The Chelsea Girls know:
the opposite of art is habit,
poetry is personality disorder,
and refusal is a leap of faith.
It is all they need
to know.

Chelsea Girls are an exchange of bad energy between
themselves
and those who briefly enter their orbit.

That orbit loops the loop:-
ceaseless macabre dancing/
bare breasts/
chewed up cunts/
fascination with secrets and arcanity –
language formed in the nightclubs
or behind bars/
a pirouette.

They are the stars
which bear crucial messages
with a Delphic code.
Baffling signals from
another smoky universe.

The Chelsea girls work as a Soho hostess.
They are a bottle of blue black hair dye,
lip pencil,
faded blue black scars,
every vein calloused.

Chelsea Girls are
an unzipped leather jacket.

Chelsea Girls monologue:
You figure out after
I'll have people around you
in London New York I like
so much dark matter you
don't know who they are
you never meet them but
they shadow you your movements
implicate one another
your good stretches and disconsolate
moment are one and the new same
the chance shifts neglected like
discarded packaging material

and some house this disconsolation
drifts out of the canal like river.

You will find their number written
in felt-tipped pen in all local phone boxes.

Chelsea Girls also say:
Fall apart, baby,
fall apart.

They cavort with naked girls
in thick woollen tights.
The comforts of nostalgia.
Always punch out kitchen door
windows at parties.
Have their best drug and sex
breakdowns in recording studios
in the Elephant & Castle.
Are filmed having their hair
being coiffured on the TV.
Throw bricks through windows
of Hells Angels' flats.
For kicks and fits.

Chelsea Girls know
that the only way
to endure existence
is to learn how to forget –
and the only way to fathom
essence is to remember.
Ah, forget it.

The Chelsea Girls know
that at the end of the night,
just like in *Dallas*,
it was all a dream.
The TV set is left

on in an empty room.
An empty hotel room.
Or, a serviced flat.
They love fluorescence,
which leaks into the ether.

They always dream
the same dream every
single night:-

lie down on the bright sad starry surface
and dream of sleep, and the dream
within that sleep:
where the place you call home
blows up – dynamite! – over and over
again in silver slo mo –
giant fireballs ripping through
the building incinerating everything,
waves of chain reaction sending contents
hurtling and spinning into
the vast open blue black night sky,
waves of power cascading through
the air towards the gaze of
the beautiful innocent dreamer
who suddenly exclaims in picturesque
dreamless ruins: *My God, I didn't realise*!

They know that at every corner
the violet shadows fall and founder,
striped with human experience,
savage and tenderly lyrical.

They hate people
who are disgusting with their eagerness
for the slightest thing.
Or, for nothing.
It goes without saying.

Chelsea Girls do not believe
that everything has to be working
all the time,
they have little belief
in the functional continuum.
They are absurd.

They give dark depression
an artistic slant.
The Chelsea Girls talk incessantly –
they know
that if they ever stop
the future will be revealed instantly.

The sound of their
famous trinket bracelets is
the jangle of bad nerves.

What do they look like?
The gaunt assemblage
of bad movies and excesses.
Like somnambulist stars
from Expressionist films.
No one wants to fuck them.

The Chelsea Girls are not Pop Art!
Rather,
a cross between cubism
and metaphysical mysticism.

They know artists must reject anything
they are attracted to.
They think you
should become your films.
You must sleep on concrete
for your posture.

The Chelsea Girls worship only
Modigliani,
who gave away his art
for a drink
or a tin of sardines...
or a handful of dust,
covering the seats of
the Scala Cinema,
London.

I know the Chelsea Girls.

The Chelsea Girls say:-

I am youth.
I am glam anti-glam positive punk.
I am bursting, full of it all.
I am 1983.
...the 80s
... the 90s
Forever.
But you just don't know it, baby.
You don't know it.
You don't know.

BRIGHT SAD STAR

Bright sad star
fell down from the sky,
but she's going back there.

Brand new,
brand now
revenge.
She was going back up there,
blazing, falling star.

The world is a heaving bucket full-to-the-brim-of dirt
with a sparse sprinkling of joy on top
– and that sprinkling is made of stardom.
They'll all be sorry.

He thought about ugliness and beauty
and how things slip through
your fingers like powder,
and wondered whether or not
he had any real sympathy for
her,
who he knew, would in the future be tiny and
exposed and at the mercy of forces
that she could never control.

Beauty will save the world, he resolved – *Idiot*.

Her thoughts were in monochrome –
giving her the feeling and pressure of
an explicit migraine.
An austere psychological aesthetic.
It all droned on in her head
nihilistically.

Bright sad star
fell down from the sky.

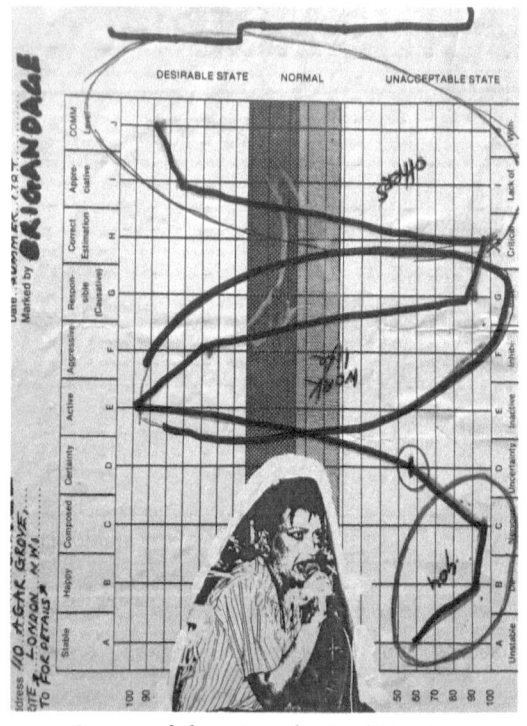

Grammar of advertising and art in which we live

FEELINGS GET BLEACHED OUT

In the Camden backstreets,
the boozers were fading testaments
to times past, and water passed
in the form of piss
up
against the proverbial wall
– and smelling much the same.

They were living in their own colourful movie
which they were sure was incomparably
richer, more spontaneous and far
more magical than the depressing,
collective dim motion-less
picture that the 9-5 conformists,
or those that stumbled around
with their booze-fuelled regrets, had to settle for.

He grinned at her – but his smile was stationary.

They're so obsessed with themselves
that they don't care about the audience

MUSIC I LISTENED TO IN MY HEAD WHILE WALKING AROUND THE JEAN-MICHEL BASQUIAT EXHIBITION AT THE LE MUSÉE D'ART MODERNE DE LA VILLE DE PARIS ON 22/01/11

... and *Edge of Blue* by DJ Krush and *Getto Skank* by Joe Gibbs and *The Art Of Rollin'* by The Mackrosoft and *Assault On Precinct* by John Carpenter and *The Beat Generation* by Bob McFadden and *Blues Montage* by Langston Hughes/Leonard Feather and *Diamonds on My Windshield* by Tom Waits and *Naked Lunch* [Excerpt] by William S. Burroughs and *The Clown* by Charles Mingus/Jean Shepherd...

... and *Game Is My Middle Name* by Betty Davis and *Wrote For Luck* by Happy Mondays and *Put Your Money Where Your Mouth Is* by Rose Royce and *The Joust* by Spectre vs. Scotty Hard and *Doze In Dub* by Bass Invaders and *Spirit Lake* by CocoRosie and *Paid In Full* by Eric B. & Rakim and *Everything Is Neu* by Hatchback Club and *Creator has a master plan* by Brooklyn Funk Essentials...

... and *Revolution Was Postponed Because of Rain* by Brooklyn Funk Essentials and *Cosmic Funk* by Lonnie Liston Smith & The Cosmic Echoes and *Me and Baby Brother* by War and *Get Fresh Boy (Dub)* by BRONXGIRLS FEAT.

CHRISSY C and *Love Don't Love Nobody* by Ella Brown and *Let Me Down Easy* by Bettye LaVette and *Requiem (Remix)* by Dr. Alex Paterson and *Dystopian Romance* by Peter Van Hoesen...

... and *Are You Experienced?* by The Jimi Hendrix Experience and *Yum Yum (Gimme Some)* by Fatback Band and *Follow the Leader* by Eric B & Rakim and *The Summer Of '42* by Gil Scott-Heron & Brian Jackson and *Shack Up* by Banbarra and *You Can't Hide From Yourself* by Teddy Pendergrass and *Give Up The Funk (Let's Dance)* by B.t. Express and *Toot An' Toot An' Toot* by Curtis Mayfield and *Double Dutch Bus* by Frankie Smith and *Fakin' Out* by The Soul Destroyers feat. Sharon Jackson...

...and *The Deafening Screams of Silence* by Hydroponic Sound System and *Big Fun (Original Mix)* by Inner City and *Hello (Boys And Girls)* by The Beloved and *I Can't Stand The Rain* by Ann Peebles and *Namaste* by Beastie Boys and *Soon Forward* by DJ Spooky and *Loop* by Ken Ishii and *Living for the City* by Stevie Wonder and *My Baby Don't Breathe* by Omar And The String poppers...

... and *Rock Billy Boogie* by Johnny Burnette and *Bottle To The Baby* by Charlie Feathers and *Talking*

Drums Whispering Vinyl by Quantic Soul
Orchestra and *Wardance* by Killing Joke
and *Keeping The Motion* by DJ
Krush and *Holly Rock* by Sheila E. and *Sucker MCs* by
Run DMC and *I Can't Live Without My
Radio* by LL Cool J and *Kung Fu Fighting* by
Lloyd Parks and *Hap Ki Do* by Big Youth and
Bon Baiser du Poste by les sages poêtes de la rue and
Green Door by WYNDER K. FROG...

... and *Why D'Ya do it* by MARIANNE
FAITHFULL
and *Snakecharmer (Francois Kevorkian Snake Dub)* by
Jah Wobble, The Edge, Holger Czukay and *Adventures
on the wheels of Steel* by GRANDMASTER FLASH
& THE FURIOUS FIVE and *Tales From Outer
Space* by Jah Wobble
and *Variations Sur un Thème de Monteverdi (I, II, III)*
by The Art Ensemble of Chicago
and *Boys Keep Swinging* by David Bowie...
... and *Bassline* by Mantronix and *Hell is Round
the Corner* by Tricky and *A Different Blues* by Apple
Juice Kid (Miles Remixed) and *Lay Down (Candles
In The Rain)*
by Melanie and *Masterpiece* by Grover Washington
Jr.
and *Riki Tiki Tavi* by Donovan and *Lazy Butterfly*
by Devendra Banhart and *Little Johnny Jewel*
by Television and *Afrodizziact* by Cry Cisco...

...and *Pretty Funny Thing* by Brigandage and *Living
In
The Ghetto* by Purple Image and *Ain't It Strange*
by Patti Smith and *Smokebelch1* by The Sabres Of
Paradise and
Let We Go (Villalobos Remix) by Rhythm & Sound
and *Skin*

I'm In by Chairmen Of The Board and *Life Is Just a Moment* by Roy Ayers and *Spliff Dub (Sukh Knight Remix)*
by Zomby ...

and *Pendulum* by DJ Krush and *The Guardian Angel Is Watching Over Us* by Golden Flamingo Orchestra and *Ghost Town* by Kode9 & The Spaceape and *Buffalo
Stance* by Neneh Cherry and *Clap your hands and stomp
your feet* by Bonni St. Claire and *Morning has broken* by Cat Stevens and *sun worshippers* by diana brown &
barrie k sharpe and *From The Heart* by Generation X and *Slang Teacher* by Wide Boy Awake...

...

GOD IN THE TYPEWRITER

He looked at the canal and saw the waterway
as a ribbon stretching not just from place to place
but as some sort of amorphous, unlimited,
unstructured time stream
– past and future –
with ambient
undercurrents of subliminal meaning
– disorienting but always in motion.

He imagined poems may not turn
out as planned in reality,
so let's leave it to
the God in the typewriter
– not to chance, but to
the turn of the page. 'OK?'

The thought of it made him
want to run away:
And if I run away,
will the words run with me?

Dilemma within society. Less than 50% that comes up to *their* standards comes up to *our* standards

SHE MIGHT HAVE BEEN AT CAFES AND BARS

Unfaithful to lovers.
With enemies like alabaster.
A face – *Pietà* By Michelangelo –
in torn photos by Philippe Halsman, André Kertész
and Hans Bellmer.
Snakelike evanescence.
She devoured them set in stone.
Inhuman never growing old.
Kickback – beautiful and as long as a weasel's back,
mesmerising victims.
Her beauty was:
the lustre of PayPal per Pearl.
Always naked but wearing violence when drunk.
Slapped unsettled sore and yawning
in a near nymphomaniacal drift.
Ivory bangles in the car lately.
Fucking feeling like snails gliding
a trail of slime over dismissive skin.
Very slim with us skaters.
What is that smell of blanched almonds?

Dramatic space – compartmentalisation of our lives, every-
where at once

LIKE IT'S ALL CONNECTED

Her subconscious moans like nothing can ever catch
fire again.
Her body cracks with longing like a reflection of
some feeling.
She is depressed like a drug that's overwhelming and
alluring.
She eats like she's scared of the thought of the smallest
detail of daily living.
She looks in the mirror like she knows all solutions
are temporary.
She wishes wish upon wish like open rebellion.
She slumps in the chair like the very meaning of
surrender.
She stays in bed with her eyes closed like she is
looking for levels beyond aesthetics.
She dances in the kitchen like there is nothing left
along cold streets.
She looks at him like it's all connected.
She argues with him like it is part of the narrative
suspense of it all.
She balances on one bare foot like she's guilty about
not feeling intensely.
She bares herself like she thinks the cultural habits of
most people make her sick.
She calculates betrayal like the enemy of all that is
vital.
She washes herself like nothing makes it easy to be
frivolous.
She Belongs Boasts Bores Burns –
like there are some surprising emotional
undercurrents
She Chokes Confesses Crosses Crushes –
like the surface is simplicity.
She disappears like a breathless victim of triumph.
She dares to drown like the embodiment of all the

73

city's regrets.

She sees ghosts in peoples' faces like a physical sensation.

She undresses like she's following a mad logic.

She understands banality like some vague somewhere, or somewhere else.

She remembers to mourn like domesticity repudiated.

She offers to suffer like identity doesn't matter.

She sends pictures of herself to people like all meaning is fluid.

She heads right at the wall, going at a hundred miles an hour, like she can't grasp her dreams.

She dreams like she pissing in a toilet bowl of full of floating cigarette ends.

ANIOŁ

When nothing remains
in the wood of your house,
the wind turns rings
in the angle of flatness,
and sand, ruins, seeps through hand.

Sutkowszczyzna settlement,
Horochów district,
Wołyńskie voivodeship.
Now void.

Sutkowszczyzna,
where
my mother,
moja matka,
nine years old,
saw with her own
flecked blue green eyes...
an angel – *anioł*.

Elemental creatures head over heels.
Devils cajole belief,
play tag with
dabs of blood.

Tempest lashes forest.
Thunder claps, hurrah!
Sheet lightening flash.
Skyline altar of the luminous.
Ghosts in sheets dancing in clouds.
Portents of tear fall,
bitter deluge.
Ghosts moving through time
– contracted and stretched
with flow of messages

from angels.
Ask them!

My mother saw the angel,
her angel or *anioł*,
looking through window, smiling.
Tall, blonde, radiant woman.
Dazzling *film star*.
Pervasive archetype and mythological motif.

'She was the most wondrous woman I ever saw,'
said awed mother eighty years in the future
to me.
'She filled me with such peace.
An angel from heaven above.'
Above primordial thoughts.

Then,
1940,
Sutkowszczyzna,
Poland.
Now,
shifting borders,
Ukraine.

Within land the magic essence,
like old poem about sense of place.
And time.
Spirals, gyres and turned earth.

Blood soaks into ground
where meaning lives.
Spirit dancers weave
where ashes remain.

Until the world ends
and keeps on ending.

Today, tomorrow
and back then.

What did dazzling Angel tell my mother?
That sun shall be turned into deepest anguish,
and the moon's craters
will fill to brim with blood splashed tears.
Pitch black,
like before there was an idea.
Those asleep in everlasting dust
will blow away.

My mother, trembling, thought:
But no dogs do
howl here.

Angel smiled at mother
and said,
I shall wail for the never bewailed.
The never bewailed.

Mother felt chillness of statues,
clouded with dark incense.
Holy smoke.
Felt shadow of future on clear widow glass.

Angel said:
but I will not
wail for you.

Now, never enough memory to contain
old women's regrets and regress
into melted lament of calamity.

Sutkowszczyzna,
a void.
Turning magical circles.

Where living help to make visions
for the dead.

Old map,
Eastern arc of fear.
Drawn over skyline overlooking
evolving horror.
As dead always think of death
in forever flashes.
Same location – call it Sutkowszczyzna,
call it void.
Map shifts, location remains.
In deep pit of war.

Lost hands of dead repeat movements
enacted again.
The energy of war
is forever damnation.
Cleansing fire of black angels
will not soothe.
Restless.

10th February, 1940,
218,000 people were
forcefully deported by the Soviets
from Eastern Poland, now Ukraine,
to Siberia.
With further deportations
during the year,
the number
rose to almost
2,000,000.

Sutkowszczyzna settlement,
Horochów district,
Wołyńskie voivodeship.
Poland.

Midnight knock on door.
My mother and her family:
up against the wall.
Bewailing.

Weeping in cattle trucks,
three weeks to the depths,
Russia,
height of winter.
No water except sobs made of icicles.
Permafrost souls,
frozen hearts.

Siberia
Arkhangelsk Oblast,
Solvychegodsk district,
Vostochno settlement.
A labour camp.

All dead and white.
Temperature dead and white.
Enveloped in dead and dark.
Bewailed place.
Dead.

Ethereal offering of ash.
A torn fragment of black silk
drifts on current
before settling into ether.

Tradition in home
where death has knocked;
drape black silk mourning ribbons
over mirrors and
all pictures depicting landscapes.

Land, with magical essence,

should not distract
the dead on final journey with
the awe of loss for ever.

Arkhangelsk Oblast,
glacial dreams.
Avalanche of solid ice.
Prismatic jewels in air mirroring
intense vast distance and
all things rigid white.
No escape.

Small mother swallowed
by shimmering anti-world.
Dead world.

We must get out of the ice forest before dark
we will make it with any luck mother wails.
Angel wails.
All bewailed.

Angel sees images of bone orchards
that we are dug into
and then out of again.

Mother dreams of home,
world moaning inside.
Land full of hallucinations,
offering signs and other weird clues.

There is dead brother Faustin,
head crushed in rotten barn.
Here comes the angry ghost.
And future ghost daughter Danuta,
head crushed in rotten English sports car.
Here's the ghost of dead future
husband, Ludomir.

He's leading a brass band up the stairs.
Wailing loud enough to wake all the dead!

Oh leave me in peace!
Mother says.

Gypsy fortune teller Lubelska way
tells old woman:
you will go far across the seas.
And never come back!
Village people who have never
even seen a city ever before,
laugh.
Just go mad.

Impossibility of return.
Eternity to wander
on land which remains
but does not retain.

Mother dreams of the dead
for the rest of her life.
Generational trauma as fever dream.
Generational memory as
shadow of trauma.

In future, I see old people's faces
in the curtains.
Harasho or *nekhorosho*?
Babcia, mother's mother, says to me each day.
I see boy in white get into coffin.
Boy is me in fever dream.

Mother wakes from and to nightmare,
weaves on path from forest,
a maelstrom,
to far horizon.

Fearful encounters
like pointers on unmapped paths.

Peril,
ruined cities,
desolate souls,
abandonment,
alone.
Always: fear.

Don't look now.
Here comes the Rusałki – ghosts of the drowned, to
seduce and carry you away.
Here comes the Południca, the noon witch to drive
you mad.
Here comes the Leshy, to lead you astray.
Here comes the Strzyga, to eat out your insides.
And Baba Yaga, face made of human bones.
Here comes the Wila, nymphs on the wind.
Here comes the Nocnica, shadow in the night, of the
night.
Disgorged by the dark psychological underground.

Here comes panic, perfidies, departures with no
arrivals,
and the opposite; upside down.

Harasho or *nekhorosho*?
Soviet labour camp soldier says to mother daily.
Answer is always
the same.

October 1941, German invasion of Russia.
Sikorski–Mayski agreement.
Mother and others given amnesty
but no home.
Land not lost but buried.

Mother dreams of home,
dances on whorls,
always tuned to odd frequencies,
listens to the dead
in Siberia's
own coils
and begins journey East.
Search for lost Polish army.

Disease.
Typhus malaria dysentery.
Crawling in blood
to open latrines.
Here comes
the devil's horses
galloping over the hill.

Starvation
that smells of remnants,
bones picked clean and
giant turtle eggs ripped
by red hands
straight from
the womb.

Windblown rumours swirl
around mother's raw feet.
War here and there.
Voices in the night.
Haunt of melancholy.

Darkness again falling – drags its covers across
country in slow moving wave.
Listen to the wind speak. Reply.
Mother knows that when you have to
live among your ghosts

you must keep the conversation flowing.

In the long cold sleep of the winter
the shapes of dead are blocked out
against moonlit sky.
Nothing moves.
Only the spirits of the place, shifting.

Dirty wind blows lights around.
Dialogue at edge of dream.
Mother seeks comfort in the stories that
voices and lights tell.

Unnameable birds shriek against the dark
that rims the sky.
Birds squall in murderous packs.
Mother dreams to escape
strange pulses.

In the East.
Heat is religious.
Pahlevi, Tashkent, Palestine.
Isfahan, to the palace of orphaned ghosts
running barefoot in night.
Mother wails *oh why did you leave me alone*?
Angel wails.
But not for her.

Typhus.
More dysentery.
Delirium.
Karkin Batasz – the Valley of Death.
Alone.
Alive.

Dark rumours now in channel of her body.
The sky now white – *shall I address my confessions to it*?

No church in Sutkowszczyzna,
only a crossroads
where mother had crossed herself.
Well, where else?

Her father, Andrzej, had made gold coins
in Brazil.
Brought them back
in treasure chest.
Kept it close.
His spells had made the world sway a little and lean
in.
And out.

Up against the wall.
Tanks on the road to Lwow, now Lviv.
Silver airplanes
in red sky.

Dead bodies laid out wrapped in sheet.
Mother looks at who had died that day.
One big grave for all.
Saw friend from Sutkowszczyzna.
Drowned in well –
others drank water unaware.
It tasted like... hell.

Mother with *jaglica* – eye disease,
Saved – off damned list – from ship of doomed
orphans
sailing Red Cross
to Mexico.
Torpedoed, all lost.
Mother crossed herself.

Mother wails.
Seeks transportation

along
non-linear narrative.
Discontinuous shards.

 Inexplicable switches between sepia and colour,
– as if this too is part of the magic.
As if indissoluble time
gives us immortality.

Slow pan of dispossessed human continuity.
Relentless whirl of frosted scarlet petals.
We are the pillaged
We do not know.
We never do.

My mother.
Hospital bed.
Cold white moon
in England
80 years in future.
Kicking hard in frenzy against death.
Now.
Now angel wails.
For the never bewailed.

I hear angel wail.
I wail.

Angel wails
for those who have been caught in
final eddy
of some great chaos
and will spin back at last to the
the wood of your house
reverting once more
into the wildest anonymity.
Call it void.

DEJA-VU, DEJA-ME, DEJA-YOU

I remember something

vivid, intense painful... untethered...
untangling life's inanity... tearing and tearing-up emptiness
(loss, lack, loss)
and existential longing...
unthinking but not vacant
– always pretty though...
and haunting... haunted...
ghostly in all senses...
and a meditation in the real sense
i.e. something that connects to a higher self
– which is a function of the sacred –
memories as a meditation on memory itself.

This, too, is a meditation.

I remember.

But the memory knots
are more like bubbles that can never be burst,
that will float forever
– like a display of abstract pop art poetry –
New York School, maybe
– 'an aesthetics of attention'
that moves the ordinary into the extraordinary
and the extraordinary into the ordinary.
The banal and the extra-banal, if you like.

Like jazz, or the freakiest rock, or dub
– it is so unrestrained and loose that
 it reminds you momentarily that you yourself are not that
– unrestrained and loose –

before inspiring and empowering
you to become *that*. Freedom. Release.

The memories are deeply fleshed,
and it's unimaginable not to be prompted
into a dialogue involving an undammed
flood of memories of our own.
A psychedelic case of
deja-vu, deja-me, deja-you.

THE CONTENTS OF DANUTA CABUT'S HANDBAG ON THURSDAY, AUGUST 23, 1973

1 brown handbag containing
Black leather purse

(£11.77 1/2. Cash. and sundry papers.
Driving licence and cert. of competence).

1 – ladies wrist watch. (broken).

1 – brown comb.

1 – ball pen.

1 – felt tip pen.

1 – tube lozenges.

1 – lipstick.

1 – small black pencil.

1 – tube 'per-fu-my'.

1 – brown compact.

1 – handkerchief.

1 – blue diary.

1 – brown envelope containing tax return forms.

1 – bunch of keys. (9) in all.

1 – one broken tablet.

+

1 pair ladies shoes.

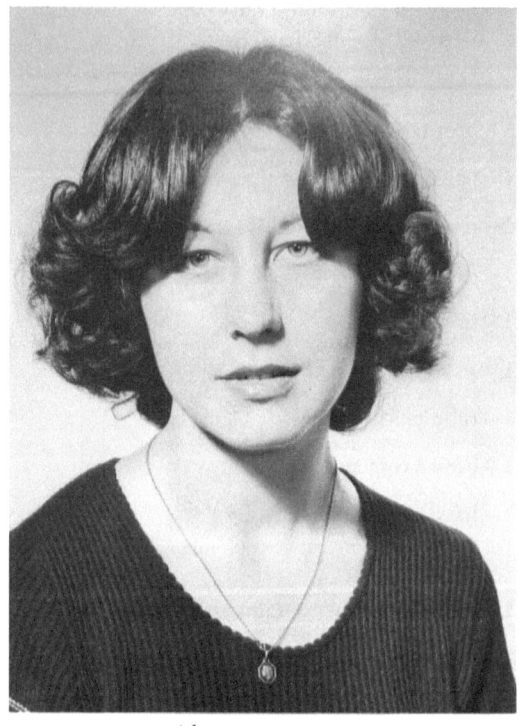

A letter sent to a sister

Father. Reality of reflection

WELL I DECLARE

Memory swirls,
mingling with dreams.
The first song I ever heard,
or remember hearing,
is *A Windmill in Old Amsterdam*
by Ronnie Hilton.
I was 5,
and the year was 1965.
The song's chorus may be familiar
to connoisseurs of the ludicrous:-

I saw a mouse!

I heard it, standing looking up,
at my parents' big old Fifties valve radio.
I was in the first floor front room,
hard grey and blue flecked linoleum on the floor,
 from where I could see my father's wardrobe.
The wardrobe door squeaked.

A little mouse with clogs on.

In that room, my parents' room,
the one with the wardrobe,
I had some years previous to hearing
A Windmill in Old Amsterdam
seen a real golly doll
– 'real' as in something forged amongst
the intricacies of consciousness.

It happened one night
– doesn't it always? –
when I awoke in my cot to find
the non-existent staring at me
through the cot bars

until my screams sent
it scuttling off to whatever
elemental, ludicrous place
– as ludicrous as the song
I now remember –
it had come from.
Maybe even across the landing
to that first floor front room,
where stood the radio.

But there it was, the valve box,
trilling out in its message,
in the same room where
only a year or so earlier
I'd seen two or three large faces
of old people in the curtains.
Their grey-haired heads looked
down quizzically on me, a little boy,
confused rather than scared by
that which shouldn't be,
perhaps?
And then, startled by a thought process
of disturbed logic, I ran to escape
and hide by a big cupboard near the landing.

Where?
There on the stair!

My mother, who had been busy scrubbing,
polishing, wiping, cooking,
worrying, sensed that
something was wrong.
In later years, when I no longer lived at home,
she would sense other
disturbances from afar,
knowing when I had been arrested, for instance.
On the day of the old people in the curtains,

she came running up the stairs to
save me from the intangible.
These things, memories or
and dreams, you carry with you.

I never did tell my mother about
the old people,
but she would have known them.
They came from the same place
as the stuff of the old Polish folk
tales she told me in my childhood.
Tales which informed me that out there

Where?

strangeness and bad magic are afoot.
In her eastern Polish village,
before being ethnically cleansed
to Siberia by the Soviets
at the start of World War II,
my mother had herself
seen the inexplicable
lights lit by the village's agitated dead,
encountered the devil's horses.
This happened.
That which does not exist.

These same stories were also told to me by my babcia,
or grandmother, who every morning,
would climb the stairs.

Going clip-clippety-clop

My babcia's Parkinson's made the cup rattle
against the saucer,
spilling some of the tea.
I would listen to this Parkinson's

cup and saucer chatter,
this strange rhythm,
and wonder why she couldn't be a little more careful.
And couldn't she be a little quicker?
Unkind thoughts in the room,
the same room where not only had I seen
the old people in the curtains,
but where I had also gone into
a dangerous coma.
My parents and a doctor gathered
around my bedside,
waiting for the ambulance when, apparently,
I sat up, pointed to a corner of the room

Right there!

and asked: 'Who is the boy in white,
the one getting into the coffin?'

I know that I had died that day,
that night, and had then come back to
haunt the present and the future forever.
I know that.

I saw a mouse!

Later, in 1978, I wondered if my grandmother,
after her death that year, and my mother,
after her own, in 2021,
had joined the other old people in the curtains.
Those old curtain people, I never saw again.
But I know they are always watching.

Nor did I hear *A Windmill in Old Amsterdam*
by Ronnie Hilton ever again after
I first heard it that first time.
And if I did hear it, I wasn't listening.
And if I was – well, I don't remember.

Well I declare!

GHOST MUSIC

I remember the house where I first heard
the song *A Windmill in Old Amsterdam*,
which even if I don't remember
hearing it ever again,
is ghost music.
And will haunt me forever.
Or at least the memory of hearing it will.

I left that house, in Ridgeway Avenue, Dunstable,
Bedfordshire, UK, behind in the 1970s
when I moved to London –
and I left it *finally*
when I locked it up for
the last time in 2021,
after everyone who had ever lived in it,
apart from me,
for the time being,
had died –
although I had died once
and came back.
First, my sister, Danuta, a pop artist,
who made graphic art
and designed cardboard furniture
(groovy times),
in 1973; my father in 2006,
and, 2020, my mother.

Now it is a ghost house
full of ghost music.
Oh yeah.

Locking up, I felt a dizziness as I went
into each empty room to say goodbye
and remember.
I envisaged the invisible trails, beams

or projections of energy
left behind, or forward,
by my family members as,
over the years, they
– we –
had moved around the house
– *à la Donnie Darko* –
these trails would be of different colours,
affected by person and mood
– like an aura –
maybe even extension of aura –
emanating and lengthening from
that person to some unknown beyond
– creating, as a by-product, nothing less than
cosmic, non-representational art
– how cool! –
the theme of which being a mixture of:
causal relationships,
dimensional constructs,
temporal paradoxes –
i.e. many versions of occurrence inhabiting
the same area –
a sense of completion
and relief and, of course,
mourning.

I remember.

As I moved around the empty but full house,
I remembered mostly
the movement and postures
 – sometimes wound into despair –
and emotional tones of my dead family
at various points of their/our arcs,
full of sadness and joy and wonder
and then horror
at events connected

with each other's achievements,
births and deaths.

I remembered the rooms as they used to be
and wondered if there is any point
in remembering the banality of furniture,
for instance – deft juxtapositions of the banal with
the revelatory –
that is exactly how the wheels of memory turn.
Simple and stupid and universal
and utterly complex.
It is the accumulation
and the rhythm and the patterns
– those colourful trails, projections and beams –
that truly depict and give meaning to our stories.

I went into the room which was
the scene of my earliest or first memory
– I am a baby in my cot, in the daytime,
alone in the room and I look around
and a fly buzzes above me.
And I cry for my mother. I cry.
And she doesn't come.

This was the last room which
I went into before I finally locked up
the house and left for home
– my current home in south London –
for the last time.
So the scene of my first memory was
the scene of the last memory
of the house,
and of one compartment
of my childhood.
And what I wanted back then
– my mother –
is exactly what I desired now.

My first memory in the house foreshadowed my last.

Memory always shadows.

I remember my first memory
– and the noise of crying,
and the design formed by tears.
Not the first tears, or the last in that house
– itself a repository, a well of tears, a hell of
grief creating its ever expanding arc of misery
within all who lived there
– hell within hell without –
a chiasmus.

This, the chiasmus that enveloped
my family after the policeman
came with news of my sister Danuta's
death, at the age of 23 on August 23rd 1973
in a car crash
 – my mother filled her hell with an infinity
of tears but never managed
to douse the flames.
I, meanwhile, 13 years old, became,
 in response, uncomfortably numb
– which is to inhabit a dark chiasmus
of a slightly different nature.

My mother did not call it grieving,
she called it existence.

Emptiness was the essence
of my own chiasmus, of course.

No feelings.
As though I was
a compliant inhabitant of
Alphaville, from Godard's film

of the same name,
where all emotions
have been outlawed.
In my own version of that movie,
I outlawed my own feelings.
Creating a dystopia of the heart.
A totalitarian state of the soul.
It was tricky for a while.
And the effects lingered.
But escape is possible.

What transforms darkness into light?
The question is asked during a cross
examination in the movie.
Answer: La *poési*.

Poetry is emotional key that
deciphers the puzzle of liberty.
The film's opening line
– *There are times when reality becomes
 too complex for oral communication* –
comes from Jorge Luis Borges' *Forms of a Legend*,
which in part elucidates
the defects of logic
– which, of course, underpins the cold,
brutal ethos of *Alphaville*.
The poetry of Borges and Paul Éluard
punctuates the film
– flares in the dark.

It releases, redeems and provokes,
it provides motion which propels
the characters out of a dead
world into a new journey.

Desire or fear are at the start,
the heart, of every journey.

And that is why in my own journey
though the Zone,
a la Tarkovsky's *Stalker*,
within the landscape of Godard's *Alphaville*,
I am perhaps the Writer.
Or, perhaps not.

Desire or fear.

What is my desire?

Desire in *Alphaville*
is punishable by death.
But surely those without desire
have already died.

It is desire that lies at
the root of the chance,
the change, the vulnerability,
and the magic which illuminates,
revealing that the chiasmus of control,
self-control, denial, self-denial, restraint
and order is an illusion.
And never mind the pain.

I remember, in the film,
Anna Karina as Natacha von Braun's
reverie-soliloquy,
the best sort of soliloquy,
an adaptation of
Paul Éluard's poem *So, What is Love, Then?*

It is transcendent. Not just her words.
Perhaps we could have done
without the words, in fact.
But the way her expression,
her physiognomy, changes from frozen

to alive and points away from the
calculated determinism that
looks at the past, present and future
as merely a consequential formula
 – one that allows no individual
thought or, yes, desire, or tears.

I looked at my own expression
in my reflection in the window of the house
and I remembered and closed my eyes softly
 – a poetic gesture, maybe, a stirring of shadows.
I wanted to float adrift.
And never mind the pain.

The house, I noticed, as I moved through it
 – and the spirit moved me? –
pulsed still with grief.
Decades.
Decades of it.
It was a construct, an assemblage, of memory and of
grief.
Memories are, of course, always both more beguiling
and dense when evoked
via a peek through the crack of
the heavy curtains of mourning.
Attunement to mortality
that leaves the vision clear.

I remember this – that.

Grief is a ghost called memory.
The gone.
Now ungone.
Haunting.

As I looked out of the window of the empty
and glacial house,

it started to snow.
Cold. No feelings.

I left the house and went into the snow.
It fell, coating me
– and I looked back one last time
at the house which had whispered me
into imagining myself at the heart of a place
where memory flows from.
Like the tears of yore
which no longer themselves flow.

But I remember the assemblage of memory
– of self and time –
which flies.
Flies but also, yes, flows
– a river cascading and sometimes
flooding around the banks of
a lost future which might have been.

The snow started to fall heavily.
I went quickly down
the path, pulling my collar up.

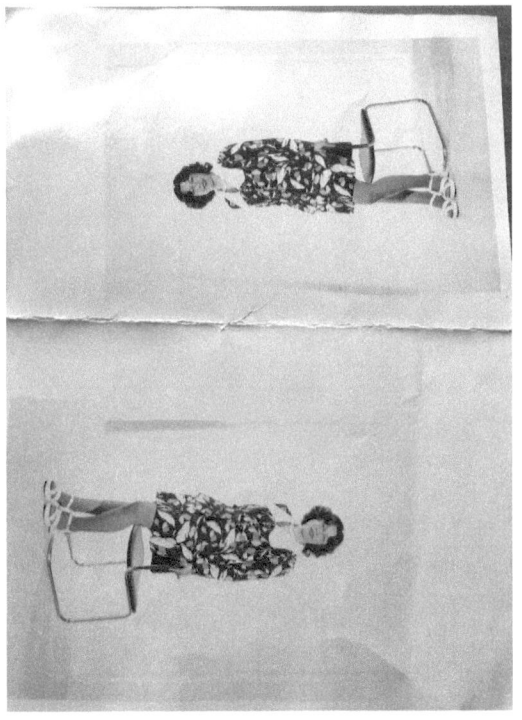

Invisible people in homes. Hidden and brilliant corners

Sur et sous le communication

REFERENCES

Disorderly Magic
– Verse 1, line 1, *Negative Girls*, Victor Bockris.
– Verse 4, line 2, *Howl*, Allen Ginsberg.
– Verse 9, lines 4-6, Verse 53, lines 2 and 8, *Performance*, Nic Roeg.
– Verse 11, lines 3-6, *Dharma Bums*, Jack Kerouac.
– Verse 14, line 2, *19th Nervous Breakdown*, The Rolling Stones.
– Verse 30, line 5-6, *Sister Ray*, Velvet Underground.
– Verse 33, lines 2-4, Janet Frame.
– Verse 40, lines 3-5, *Break it Up*, Patti Smith.
– Verse 48, line 6, *Little Ghost*, Max/Leslie Winer.
– Verse 55, lines 4-9, *Stolen Kisses* (1968), François Truffaut.

Thoughts while watching Chelsea Girls at the Scala Cinema, London, on Saturday 10th September, 1983
– Verse 1, lines 3 and 4, *Heroin*, The Velvet Underground.
– Verse 2, line 6, *Chelsea Girls*, Nico.
– Verse 4, line 4, *I'll Be Your Mirror*, The Velvet Underground.
– Verse 13, line 2, *I'm Waiting For The Man*, The Velvet Underground.
– Verse 49, lines 3-6, *Emotional Rescue*, The Rolling Stones.
– Verse 54, lines 6 and 7, Don't Look Over Your Shoulder, but the Sex Pistols are Coming, *New Musical Express*, Neil Spencer.
– Verse 75, line 5, *Anarchy In The UK*, the Sex Pistols.
– Verse 80, line 4, *Chelsea Girls*, Nico.
– Verse 100, line 4, *Mannequin*, Wire.
– Verse 105, line 4, the Cowboys t-shirt, Vivienne Westwood and Malcolm McLaren.
– Verse 114, lines 2 and 3, 1970, *Fun House*, The Stooges.

Tenth Floor
– Verse 3, line 8, *Freedom's Plough*, Langston Hughes.
– Verse 7, line 3, *The Holy Barbarians*, Lawrence Lipton.
– Verse 9, line 11, *Search And Destroy*, Iggy and the Stooges.

Bright Sad Star
– Verse 5, *The Idiot*, Fyodor Dostoyevsky.

Aniol
– Verse 6, line 5, *Ask The Angels*, Patti Smith.

INDEX AND POEM OF FIRST LINES

SELECT BIBLIOGRAPHY

Loitering With Intent – Muriel Spark
Jumpin' Jack Flash – Keiron Pim
Never Come Morning – Nelson Algren
Contemporary – Lesley Jackson
The Serial – Cyra McFadden
About Collage – Peter Blake
The Lost Weekend – Charles R Jackson
The Year Of Magical Thinking – Joan Didion
New York City In 1979 – Kathy Acker
Guy Debord: Complete Cinematic Works – Ken Knabb (ed.)
Performance – William Hughes
Wormwood Star: The Magickal Life Of Marjorie Cameron – Spencer Kansa
I Read The News Today, Oh Boy – Paul Howard
Torpor – Chris Kraus
Funeral Rites – Jean Genet
The Book Of Disquiet – Fernando Pessoa
Regarding The Pain Of Others – Susan Sontag
Godard: Images, Sounds, Politics – Colin McCabe
Only Lovers Left Alive – Dave Wallis
The Chain Of Chance and Solaris – Stanisław Lem
Steps – Jerzy Kosinski
America – Jean Baudrillard
The Witkiewicz Reader – Daniel Gerould (ed.)
The Beauty Queen Of Leenane – Martin McDonagh
Collected Screenplays – Andrei Tarkovsky
A Chemical Romance – Jenny Fabian
9 – Andrzej Stasiuk
Ringolevio – Emmett Grogan
Savage Messiah – Laura Oldfield Ford
The Hidden Files – Derek Raymond
Dangerous Parking – Stuart Browne
The Hour Of The Star – Clarice Lispector
Vernon Subutex: Volume 1 – Virginie Despentes
Walking Through Clear Water In A Pool Painted Black – Cookie Mueller
Metamorphoses – Ovid
The Birthday Party – Harold Pinter
Roman Tales – Alberto Moravia
The Master And Margarita – Mikhail Bulgakov
Heroin – Ann Marlowe
Cosmos – Witold Gombrowicz
My Year Of Rest And Relaxation – Ottessa Moshfegh
The Motel Life – Willy Vlautin
Ithell Colquhoun – Amy Hale
Negative Girls – Victor Bockris
Waiting For Godot – Samuel Beckett
Patrick Melrose – Edward St Aubyn

Been Down So Long It Looks Like Up To Me –Richard Fariña
Two Tracts On Cartomancy – Austin Osman Spare
Pandora's Handbag – Elizabeth Young
Tales Of Beatnik Glory – Ed Sanders
House Of The Angels – Timothy Wilson
Speed Queen – Stewart O'Nan
Young Adam – Alexander Trocchi
Outside The Circles Of Time – Kenneth Grant
Widow Basquiat – Jennifer Clement
A Violent Life – Pier Paolo Pasolini
Pink – Gus Van Sant
Short History Of Decay –EM Cioran
Time Regained – Marcel Proust
Voyage In The Dark – Jean Rhys
Oleanna – David Mamet
A Lover's Discourse – Roland Barthes
Dandy In The Underworld – Sebastian Horsley

CREDITS AND ACKNOWLEDGEMENTS

Heartfelt thanks to: Willie Crane, Simone Stopford, Sandy Wilson, Gregory Hesse, Sylvie Selig, Laura Board and, of course, the good reader. Salut!

This book was written largely to accompaniment of the radio shows: *Cold War Happy Hour, Bad Punk, Spiritmuse, Cosmic Odyssey, Explorations In Dub*.

AUTHOR BIOGRAPHY

Richard Cabut is author of the novels *Looking for a Kiss* (PC-Press, 2023. Previous edition: Sweat Drenched Press, 2020) and *Dark Entries* (Cold Lips Press, 2019), co-editor/-writer of the anthology *Punk is Dead: Modernity Killed Every Night* (Zer0 Books, October 2017), contributor to *Ripped, Torn and Cut – Pop, Politics and Punks Fanzines From 1976* (Manchester University Press, 2018) and *Growing Up With Punk* (Nice Time, 2018).

His journalism has featured in the *Guardian*, the *Daily Telegraph*, *NME* (pen name Richard North), *ZigZag*, *The Big Issue*, *Time Out*, *Offbeat* magazine, the *Independent*, *Artists & Illustrators* magazine, *thefirstpost*, London Arts Board/Arts Council England, *Siren* magazine, etc.

Other fiction has appeared in the books *The Edgier Waters* (Snowbooks, 2006) and *Affinity* (67 Press, 2015). As well as on various internet sites.

He was a Pushcart Prize nominee 2016.

Richard's plays have been performed at various theatres in London and nationwide, including the Arts Theatre, Covent Garden, London.

His poetry has appeared in *An Anthology of Punk Ass Poetry* (Orchid Eater Press, 2022), and magazines such as *Cold Lips*, *Foggy Plasma*, *3:AM Magazine*, etc.

Richard exhibited as contributing artist (textual) to *Always On My Mind*, an exhibition in aid of The National Brain Appeal, the Fitzrovia Gallery, London, July 2022.

He published the fanzine *Kick* (1978-1982), and played bass guitar for the punk band Brigandage (LP *Pretty Funny Thing* – Gung Ho Records, 1986).

richardcabut.com

ALSO OUT ON FAR WEST

farwestpress.com

+1 (541) FAR-WEST